DEVIL AMONG THE TAILORS

SIMON CURTIS

Shoestring Press

Printed by imprintdigital
Upton Pyne, Exeter
www.imprintdigital.net

Typeset by narrator
www.narrator.me.uk
enquiries@narrator.me.uk

Published by Shoestring Press
19 Devonshire Avenue, Beeston, Nottingham, NG9 1BS
(0115) 925 1827
www.shoestringpress.co.uk

First published 2011

ISBN 978 1 907356 42 1

ACKNOWLEDGEMENTS

Grateful acknowledgements to *Acumen, Assent, Dorset Yearbook, Interpreter's House, London Magazine, Other Poetry, Poetry Nottingham,The Spectator* and *The Thomas Hardy Journal* where some poems first appeared. 'Satie at the End of Term' was in the new Oxford and Penguin Books of Light Verse; 'Dorchester Pastoral' in *Speaking English, Poems for John Lucas* (now retitled 'Dorchester Rural'); and 'Gym' was commended in the Bridlington Philip Larkin Poetry Competition.

A few of the poems are reprinted from *On the Abthorpe Road* (Davis Poynter, 1975), *Sports Extra* (Littlewood, 1988), *The Chronometer* (Paper Bark Press, Sydney, chapbook, 1990) and *Spike Island Spring* (Shoestring Press chapbook, 1996), all of which are out of print.

Cover image: 'White Peonies' (1969) by Susan Curtis.

For Carole

I think the groundhog'd like to chew
A fresh-baked saffron bun from Looe
Or, even better, two.
– *Email to Maine*

Contents

COMET OVER GREENS NORTON

Binoculars focusing true
(Ten o'clock from Cassiopeia),
I pick out Hale-Bopp – head, coma and tail –
Its sky-smudge icicle-clear,

Remote over Allibone's farm
On its orbit hurtling away,
And due to return from the depths of space
In four thousand years, so they say;

As far ahead as Homer is back,
Two million calendar days.
To focus true on time-scales like that
Unnerves to the quick as I gaze,

Stood at midnight on Blakesley Hill
In the frost by a neighbour's fence.
What on earth will Hale-Bopp look down on,
Four millennia hence?

CARPE DIEM

Place Aristide-Briand, Thonon

In memory of Julian Pianta-Snelling

Mathieu climbs into the mauve spaceship,
Gripping the steering-wheel tight;
As the roundabout starts to go round,
He's brought into and then out of sight.

At a café table, we're sat close by
And wave each time he appears;
Tunes the roundabout's sound-system plays
Are out-of-date by fifty years,

Post-World War Two accordion stuff –
That's back to our childhood, we laugh.
Crouched in his cockpit, the boy doesn't care
(Well, he's only three and a half);

Entirely engrossed in his own here-and-now,
He shows how to seize the day
To us *loco parentis* sixty-year-olds
In a pretty exemplary way.

SNOW GEESE

Snow geese came into view like a kept promise
– William Fiennes

It wasn't the image of snow geese
Way up in the blue Dakota sky
Migrating north toward Canada
His words sparked off in my inner eye,

But more what his simile implied
Of a preordained scheme of things:
Snow geese in Vs, like a promise kept,
With a following wind at their wings,

Where man is one with nature and part
Of some higher determining law –
Set free from self-doubt's self-questionings –
Inevitable, driven and sure.

PASTORAL

A yellow JCB
Is flailing hedgerows bare
On the road by Kingthorn Mill.
Hoarse revving sours the air

As wood is skived raw white
In a slashing wholesale rip
Of this September's store
Of blackberry, rose-hip,

Haw, elder, honeysuckle
And pale blue early sloes;
The cost-effective way
That husbandry now goes.

No joke to see the scathe
Of this familiar lane
I've known for forty years –
Though flailers, raising Cain

To standardise each hedge
With teeth of tempered steel,
Make clear to pastoralists
What farm work is for real.

WINTER FLOWERING

Planted by previous owners,
And entirely new to me,
It's a kind of amaryllis –
Nerine bowdenii –

Which, programmed by its DNA,
Must bloom from bulb or corm
Into midwinter British murk
And not midsummer warm;

'Spidery icing-sugar-pink'
The gardening handbook says;
Perverse and girly and forlorn
In raw east wind like today's.

THE HARRISON-KENDALL CHRONOMETER (K1)

'Our never-failing guide' Cook called it –
The brilliant Kendall chronometer;
For with Greenwich time fixed for three long years,
He knew what he owed the inventor:

Those longitude bearings, essential to chart
A voyage that would alter the earth,
As in oceans unmapped as outer space,
Untested but true, K1 kept faith.

Science it was, then, followed the flag,
With the urge to know and discover
Flowing natural as the Pacific tides
Astern of the Bark *Endeavour;*

So if, from some dead ground, poet,
You mark Carina or Southern Cross
As emblems of sense of estrangement,
Of human littleness or loss,

Then consider the fixed Meridian,
Chronometer, sextant and stars;
Think how what's measurable may offer
Its own propitious metaphors,

Like the gravity-pull of Reason –
Wherein readings from light-points provide
Facts for the skilled to work on and chart,
For those who may follow, a guide.

A FEW SUPERLATIVES

The Mersey valley starts at Cheadle Heath,
Where steep streets climb and, timeworn, terrace-rows
Clad primal rock with brick, and at whose foot
The dirtiest river in all Europe flows.

Our city likes to boast superlatives:
The biggest campus; football team the best;
Slum clearance tops; new shopping mall A1;
Add in the Mersey, then. The dirtiest.

We've humour, though, to compensate for all
That chemical and acid toxin stew;
Pollution there so dire, our river rates
Fire-hazard listing – in that rarest, too.

I walked there on a wet-through day last week;
Two horses browsed a dingy urban lea
Near pylon and dead willowherb and gorse –
Their chestnut coats as rich as rich could be.

CRUNCH

I try to fathom how it works:
How risk's secured via packaged debt,
A form of asset traders trade
Through SIV and CDO.
And then there are derivatives,
Which sound like supercharged roulette,
Options and futures – place your bet.
What point in thrift, frugality,
In long-term savings, meant to grow,
When money's cheap and interest low,
With credit's Big Bang go, go, go?

Ask analysts at Citigroup,
Ask Bank of England, ask the Fed,
Do market fundamentals still
Comprise a culture you can trust?
What happens, say, when loans fall due?
If Wall Street trading screens turn red
Alarming days could lie ahead.
I try to fathom how it works –
Short-selling, hedge-funds and the rest –
Then hear the breaking news (you've guessed)
As, one by one, the banks go bust;

Bear Stearns and Lehman, B & B,
Glitnir and Fortis, Northern Rock …
Words like freefall, meltdown, slump,
Mean balance-sheets all shot to hell.
Ask laissez-faire free marketeers
Why Alan Greenspan, taking stock,
Expressed his disbelief and shock?

I try to fathom how it's turned
To fuck-up on a whopping scale –
Deregulation's Holy Grail
A grand illusion. Verdict: fail.

NORTH AND HILLARD

Lay siege (that's *obsidere*); make a breach;
Or man the walls and barricade the gate;
In serried ranks, let cohort troops lay waste
And cause great slaughter as they subjugate …

In North and Hillard's true blue *Latin Prose,*
Across a gap of nearly five decades,
I re-read sentences I struggled with
For Common Entrance, then O level grades;

Bellum administrare and so on,
And grammar rules which seemed immutable –
No daily life, no childhood, schooldays, love,
Decidedly no poetry at all.

How could they have approved of Horace, who
Had flung away his shield at Philippi?
Then, amnestied, lived on his Sabine farm
To write with tolerant urbanity

Of country life, of sane, realistic hopes –
And girls and friendship and Caecuban wine –
Both wary of imperial politics
And all too well aware of fleeting time.

And what he wrote endured two thousand years,
That shrewd, ironic and Horatian tone,
Which (oh my education!) I was forced
To seek out and discover on my own.

FOINAVON

That great day when at Aintree
  Foinavon came in first –
the National also-ran,
  the dud, the hopeless case –
while the crowd, astonished, gaped,
  and all the punters cursed,
we knew that for once we'd seen
  a miracle taking place;

you double bézique, sheer fluke,
  you royal flush, blind luck,
you treble chance come right,
  you pawn who took the queen,
you Cinderella tale,
  you swan once ugly duck,
five-hundred-to-one wild guess,
  and black renegade thirteen;

you bullion found in the attic,
  you legacy hope come true,
you hit, you hole-in-one,
  you random long shot star,
what worlds of incredible chance
  will find their mark in you –
Foinavon, galloping home,
  when things that we dreamt of, are.

SNAP

In the snap I took of you
At Little Morton Hall,
You looked extremely brassed off,
Worn down, it seems, by it all;

Hand from the wheelchair arm-rest
Upraised as for form's sake,
In a glum salute on this,
Our special May Day break;

Grasping your ice-cream cone
(A double, raisin and rum)
As, son and carer, I coax
'Let's have a photo, Mum!'

Neither the old, eccentric,
Endearingly lop-sided
Half-timbered, moated house –
Which should have delighted –

Nor the solicitous guides
Could really help at all
That damp grey May Day noon
To raise our joint morale.

We each knew perfectly well
How we'd tried our level best;
Let's drive back to the Home,
You said, even that, and rest.

IN ST FIMBARRUS CHURCH, FOWEY

In memoriam VSMC

This was (so says a small brass plate)
Sir Arthur Quiller-Couch's seat;

Anthologist and novelist
And Lloyd George party loyalist,

Yacht Club Commodore and Mayor.
Who held the Cambridge English Chair.

*

I've come in for a moment's break,
Reflection and remembrance sake,

To kneel to say a prayer for you,
Close to that staunch old liberal's pew;

(His *Oxford Book of English Verse*
A well-known text to you, of course –

An Eng Lit undergraduate
In long-gone 1928).

And how you would have chuckled, too,
To think of Quiller-Couch – of 'Q';

Your laughter, I remember that,
As I begin. *Requiescat.*

GYM

A *thud thud thud* of running on the spot,
As trainers pound out dogged treadmill miles;
Below the gym's steel air-conditioning ducts,
We focus on vague distance. No one smiles.

My heart-rate read-out reads red one-one-six –
Ten minutes pounding gone, ten more to go;
A fifty-something woman in gold specs
Slides on a cable-rower to and fro.

In what looks like a virtual Tour de France,
Two youths, head down, pump legs on bike-machines;
A chap with sideburns flexes dumbbell flies;
A girl does fitball squats in cut-down jeans.

A bank of TV screens, the volume off,
Relays some golf, a chat show and the news;
Adductors, hamstrings, triceps, biceps, pecs –
We pay the health-gods' sweaty work-out dues,

And exercise just like automatons,
Our faces glum, oh fit to bust a gut,
As men think six-pack abs and women dream
Of slimmer hips and shapely bust and butt.

Get bio-rhythms right, boost self-esteem,
That fitter, leaner, greener goal in view;
This England; work-life balance and less stress –
Heart-rate in red's now up to one-four-two.

MECHANICAL NIGHT CLUB BRONCO

They say girls ride it topless some nights, too.
Well, they deserve a medal, that's my view;

Just picture it – . Try not to, then. At all.
Cold shower. Cross-country run. Miss Greer. St Paul.

An atavistic British LCM
Where male gaze stalks. One should, of course, condemn.

But she agreed to it, you can't deny …
They made her. She's a victim … Don't see why;

It's the world and its fancy (not its wife) …
It's bad … It could be worse. It's Freud. It's life.

These things go on, so take them in good part?
It's hard to focus once the broncoes start.

CANAL, HIGH LANE

What warmed, I suppose, was the *thought* of heat –
Touched randomly off by the coaly fumes
Which blew my way on a bitter east wind
As I stood near a lock, numb to the bones –

A narrow-boat passing, crunching through ice
(*Lark* on its cabin in curlicued gold),
Whose chimney's black smoke for an instant seemed,
By a trick of sense, to abate the cold.

The sour tang worked its perceptual sleight,
If not quite a world from a grain of sand,
Then warmth out of freeze, improbably real –
Mind over matter, or the other way round.

A schedule to keep, the *Lark* passed from sight.
Cracked ice, as it settled, glittered with light.

AT BELLINGHAM

Out from the peat-brown waters,
Mayflies are starting to hatch,
Eddying wing-beat blurs of white
The fresh cross-breezes catch,

Causing the pale twilight specks
To appear to drift and dither,
As they couple, conceive and, spent,
Fall back to reeds or river.

Primeval forms, the mayflies teem,
Renewed once again into flight
Like flakes in a flurry of snow,
Bizarre in June half-light –

Leaving the two of us torn
Between enchantment and grief;
Thrilled by their epiphany,
Aware, though, just how brief

These lives, so soon effaced;
Such beauty and such waste.

GIFT

A fiver each for the children;
A small 'dab in the fist', I say –
Using a phrase you used to use
Which, now that you've passed away,

Takes on a new significance,
Like something by chance left behind.
How your clear-cut inflexion of voice
Comes vividly back to mind.

CLICHÉ

'It's not the end of the world', I said
To the check-out girl as I paid,
On finding out that my loyalty card
Was not in my wallet, mislaid.

The old cliché I used with a shrug
Might have been better thought through,
The morning after the one that had been
The end of the world for you.

PROM

It's Constant Lambert's *Rio Grande,*
Live tonight from the Albert Hall;
A piece you loved but for me fresh ground;
I switch on my new digital –

The first Proms season since you died,
And, irony, your birthday date;
As the players start to hit their stride,
I listen like a surrogate.

SEAFRONT CAFÉ BAR

On the terrace, an elderly couple
Sit wordless at coffee together,
With apparently nothing on earth
That they want to say to each other.

There's a widower, too, with his paper
(And crossword for something to do)
With lots he would like to talk over,
But no one to tell it all to.

FACE VALUE

The seaside rough sleepers, three of them, move
On a shine of sand in clear silhouette –
Their bags and bedrolls left in a heap
On foreshore shingle above tideline wet –

Competing at skimming stones out to sea,
Joshing together and making high fives,
As carefree as kids, or a seeming so,
To take at face-value three glimpsed lives.

PRODUCER THEATRE

Enter Autolycus, wheeling a Vespa;
She'd a punk hair-do, was wearing a parka,

And spoke Glaswegian Scots, to boot.
The audience thought it all a great hoot.

Innovative, bold, whatever you will –
But what space was left for *acting* to fill?

PHOTOGRAPH OF THE ARTIST

Anag-rhyme poem

Seeing him so, stiff as a ramrod,
Glaring and bearded, who would demur
With such a gruff bank-manager?
Oh sure, his regimen
Is facts, curt speech, plain words; for see
How man-to-man the straight eye is.
A stickler for the system, yes …

But look below: the caption says Matisse.

Though expectations lead you on
You cannot tell from looks, oh no.
This ramrod man was colour's lover;
With what light heart he'd joy and revel
In frank large shapes and sensuous line;
How finely his bright nudes stretch or kneel.

Our automatic labels
The photograph belies.
Intent on the outward, we may well lose
The nature of the artist's soul.

Mark what a midget Keats was, under five foot.
And Byron at one time was a sixteen stone tough.

SATIE AT THE END OF TERM

The mind's eye aches from Henry James,
Like arms from heavy cases, lugged for miles.
  Theme and structure, imagery and tone.

From Lawrence, too; how hard I dug
For insights sunk, yards deep, in turgid prose.
  Theme and structure, imagery and tone.

Web of necessity in *Daniel Deronda,*
Gloom in *Dorrit,* gloom in Flaubert,
One more week to go, at
  Theme and structure, imagery and tone.

So fitful-fresh as April sun,
You're welcome, clown;
Your good melodic dissonance
Will pierce low clouds of syllabus
  With humour's grace,
  Mercy of irreverence.

DARKLING THRUSH - BOCC*

An amber alert's been announced on behalf
Of various species of bird,
And it includes the storm-cock mistle thrush,
The fellow that Hardy once heard.

It's not so un-Hardy-like, too, to reflect
As New Year's glasses are clinked,
That some ninety-nine years since he penned his piece,
His mistle might soon be extinct.

Though when the song's gone, we'll conjure it up
On CD or the internet;
In a technical way, we'll be able to cope –
Log on and tune into it yet,

As an echo, like virtual hope.

**Birds of Conservation Concern*

THE GLEBE

For Andy and Fi

Our moon-cast shadows slither as we climb
Across the chill white glebe toward the house.
Like icy jewels, yet moving, ceaseless, look!
You point the Pleiades, then Sirius.

Through ground set harling-hard, the Quair swirls on;
Trout in its freezing flow, alert still, mark
Vibrations from our boots at thirty feet,
And flick in fright from deep to deeper dark,

The dog sixth-senses movement we can't see.
And stops, ears pricked. Who's there? Who's watching? Stares?
A *qui vive* earth – apart, on edge, all nerves –
Stakes out what we call ours, the trespassers.

EGG

I could hear a youth in the passing car
Guffaw with his mates as he chucked the egg,
Fantastically funny, oh ha ha ha,
When it hit me, *splat,* knee-high on the leg.
My cords sticky-smeared with wet from the yolk,
I'd become, on my way to the pub that night,
The butt of some morons' practical joke,
Aware of the threat in their whoops of delight
As their car roared off past a thirty sign.

I don't know what Plymouth is coming to –
It happened last week to a friend of mine –
The landlady said in the *Fortescue,*
As she kindly produced a warm damp cloth
To wipe the goo and bits of eggshell off.

GOLDFISH

I looked one morning and the lot had gone,
The dozen goldfish in my backyard pond;
The cull occurred one cold spell icy day.
It must have been the seagulls scoffed them all –
Were famished, probably, so *zap*. And *zap*.
The tabby cat from two doors down the street.
Who sometimes stalked the pond, was suspect, too,
Although I doubt he'd catch all twelve in one.
Odds on the seagull then. I'd plied the fish
With koi sticks daily (vitamin-enhanced),
And forked out fifty quid to pay for help
To change the water and clean out the pond –
Made out of fibreglass, ten foot by four.
Can't say I loved the fish, but did my bit;
They swam and jinked or hung about, gold-lithe,
Among the slimy lily stems and leaves.
I thought of films on Darwin on TV,
The struggle for existence and the rest,
How even in suburban Mannamead
It's dog eats dog in nature, so to speak:
A dozen goldfish down a gull's gullet.
I looked one morning and the lot had gone.

SORTING THE PAPERS OUT

Words of marital strife and hurt
In letters found by chance, and read,
Can't help but touch and disconcert,
Though those involved are all now dead.

High time to bin the letters, so
The pain at last is locked away
For good from sixty years ago?
I don't think kin should have to pay

Such bygone sorts of family debt.
Forbearance, then. Forgive. Forget.

BLACKTHORN

On some rough by the oil refinery
  Where the road bisects Ellesmere Port,
Through the car's nearside window my eye
  Was for a split second caught

By blackthorn out, in patches, silver-pale –
  Then a road-bridge, GUINNESS – and gone.
So with thoughts dead-set on their short-term goal
  (The journey, foot down, get on),

Delight, when it stirred, came nagged, as it were,
  By a kind of pulled tendon hurt;
The not having bothered that much this year,
  The not having stayed alert.

PLYMOUTH VIGNETTE

You can see 'Beryl Cook moments' everywhere
– Jess Wilder

In memory of Beryl Cook

The Dial-a-Dog-Wash van's appeared,
With loads of dog-wash stuff on board,
To strike in our suburban street
A likeably absurdist chord.

With k-swiss trainers on her feet,
The dog-wash girl pads up the path
To sort the pooch at number eight.
Shampooing? Grooming? Hydro-bath?

In Mutley Plain a pincher's booked
To have its ID Microchip
And up Eggbuckland way a peke
Is due for Flea Rinse and a Clip.

She's got a busy schedule, then;
A sly half-smile plays on her lips;
Her white snug-fitting jeans reveal
A plump backside and curvy hips –

At ease in big pink trainers, look,
A figure out of Beryl Cook.

DORCHESTER RURAL

Bridleway and beech-trees,
With robin-song and rook,
And sloes and old man's beard
In hedgerows, too – but look:

Below the wooden footbridge,
Front bumper in the stream,
A burnt-out joyride Peugeot
Mucks up both mood and theme;

In Indian summer sun,
Faint skeins of cirrus high,
The hatchback dumped and torched –
For heaven's sake, just why?

Schadenfreude impulse?
Binge drinking dare? Or joke?
Excess testosterone?
Amphetamines or coke?

Twenty thousand poundsworth
Of high spec tech gone west;
So much for Barnes's Dorset,
And all the rural rest.

SIGNS

The brand new industrial units
at the side of the M61
with steel cladding panels all painted
postmodernist dove-grey and plum,

are showing the effects already
of weathering's wear and tear;
a mould of moss by a down-spout,
and fresh rust-streaks here and there.

There's a notice on some of them, too,
To Let with Vacant Possession;
state of the art, the premises,
state of the world, recession.

For those with an eye for such things
(and a summary way with rhymes),
a townscape to note as symbolic.
an ironical sign of the times –

except that I think of John Galvin,
my friend, and of Mary, his wife;
John who built his building firm up
throughout the best years of his life,

till interest rates went through the roof,
and investment dropped through the floor,
so that client and subcontractor
couldn't meet their bills any more.

So when the bank refused him a loan,
the poor fellow went under and all,
and ironic's not quite the right term
for a friend gone like that to the wall.

While those with an eye for such things
may read subtexts in townscape, and spiel,
they remind me too much of my friend,
and what he and his missus must feel;

of how signs are just signs in the end,
at a zillion removes from the real.

G.W.

I hated you at first; slowly
Ploughing through a thick *Selborne*
One stuffy April in the library,
Five dilatory page an afternoon,

Split up by coffee breaks hour long,
While thoughts in poker game got spent
To stave off reading further on
About just where ring ouzels went

In spring, how swallows' nests were built;
(Oozal or owsal, quipped my pen,
Among notes accreting slow as silt);
The whitethroat, chiffchaff, willow-wren –

So dottle-dry, compared to dice!

But things I came to prize, in time;
To see in shadows, bright as lace,
The crowfoot star a Berkshire stream,

Or the blue gleam of a damselfly
By flooded oyster beds one May,
Where curlews haunt with keening cry,
Or, surprised, catapult away,

Wings frantic, necks outstretched in fear.
Across the ebbing estuary.

Perceptions teenage crude, these fade
Compared to your keen eye, sixth sense,
Which sparked them, secretly. You made
Your village compass rich as France.

AFTERMATH

A new day followed, coldly, on
Our grief-day's burial adieus –
With Robin in the steading yard
Out working with his blackface ewes,
Robustly, by the dip's green slosh,
Dunking the creatures, one by one.
Though yesterday was obsequies,
Today is jobs that must be done.

HOPKINS AT ST BEUNO'S

'Enough for a patch on a Dutchman's trousers',
You remark of the clouds' small skylight of blue,
As, shying away from expecting too much,
We gaze from St Beuno's at Hopkins's view;

And then spot a kestrel, windhovering high –
The chance like some grace note of natural life
To claim as good fortune in a perspective
We share, I don't doubt, with the world and its wife.

Distrusting transcendence, all Hopkins perceived
Of Unity, Being and Creation *per se,*
Don't we sell his belief and his vision short
In our sceptical, twentieth century way?

The miracles, too, at St Winefride's Well
(Where Catholic and recusant pilgrims have come
To celebrate Mass, or to bathe and be healed,
Continuously over a millennium)

That led him to write of the spring water's 'stress',
As it brimmed and reflected God-given skies;
The Well was no grace note but manifest sign
Of imminent, unfailing Grace to his eyes.

And we know off by heart so much that he wrote,
For all it subverts our refractory view;
A hawk which we happened to spot, then was gone,
And the clouds' coincident patch of pure blue.

LEAVING TOWCESTER VICARAGE

Up and down the stairs, with clump of boot on board,
The Pickfords men moved items, one by one;
We talked of football with them over tea –
The Hesketh bike, and what the Council'd done
About its car-park scheme – phlegmatically,
As if nothing untoward;
Sat round the table this time, though, we knew
Beyond the door there, in the stone-flagged hall,
The books had gone, no Cruikshank on the wall …
The Cobblers start next season up at Crewe.

Keep busy now, and don't give in to gloom;
I take my matches out, and then crouch down
To set alight the mildewed leather box
Of juvenilia I've dumped on the brown
Dry earth, where iceberg roses and mauve phlox,
Serene as ever, bloom.
Then the acrid blue smoke-ribbons rise;
While cool Madonna lilies in their row
Next to the limestone wall, as ever, glow,
A past's detritus disperses to the skies.

The town-hall chimes, the church bell just behind,
The 'synagogue' you won't lock any more.
Its tolls, its quarter-peals, the eight o'clock,
And big Vic Burt who rang them, strict as law,
Blacksmith and verger, gone. How much comes back,
Bewildering, to mind!
Old Cyril Buckland's hand-cranked roundabout

One damp June garden fete I helped to run;
His wedding, with white horses and a brougham!
Like me, he's balding now, and getting stout.

Foxed pages of old registers recall
The seventeenth century names we know –
Dunkley, Loveridge, Allen and Linnell,
Father to son to son, unfolding slow
Succession in the town, soul after soul,
Each individual;
The parsons' scripts mark, birth by birth, each name,
Yet telescoped as in a wink of time;
Revs Lockwood, Roper, Ford, now you. That chime's
Rung out each day, three centuries, the same.

How we would listen to Mum's Delius,
Together on the drawing-room settee,
Two teenage boarding schoolboys there, all ears!
Like yesterday, it all comes back to me,
Though you've not sat to play in recent years –
That's what arthritis does.
And beds undug, well, what's the point, you say,
We're off, we've grubbed up roots and bulbs to take
For the 'box' we've bought – then, quietly, make
Your joke, it's a box we end up in, anyway.

Things helped to mar the last few months we had;
Those plans to sell the house – *as offices!*
They thought, the Goths, they'd get a new one built;
And sited in the garden, if you please!
That Canon Urquart in it to the hilt;
A stinker, and quite mad.
The PCC, thanks goodness, threw it out –

The church is stuffed with bland committee men,
Who'd join the Baptists, outlaw Series One;
None of them's an earthly what it's all about.

And one last time I wander round the side
Along the passage we shot airguns in
To have a pee (old force of habit still)
By outhouse fete flags, folding chairs, the bin,
Then leave, no looking back, by strength of will
To shrug off what has died.
And pegs still on the line – so normal, all –
Under the beech whose grape-dark August leaf
Lent relish to the heart yet, crossed by grief;
Short tenancy of richness; leaves must fall.

I called in at Cold Higham afterward,
Where my nephew and my niece were staying,
She engrossed in the *Boy Friend's* film remake
He with a frisbee in the garden playing.
We spoke of school, swapped jokes, I tried to shake
Dismay off – word by word.
I'll not scythe nettles down again below
The apple-tree tangle, or feast my eye
On our yew and copper-beech. And so, goodbye.
Soon on that bonfire ash, new grass will grow.

CONTINUUM

The 'Devil Among the Tailors'; the old folk tune,
Which a fiddler, busking, played
In Stockport's Merseyway, near Asda and Monsoon,
Echoed through the mall's postmodern glass arcade.

I recognised the air, reminded, like some cue,
How back in the eighteen-forties,
The tune was a favourite in Hardy's Dorset, too –
Or so he commented in one of his stories –

Not that the young Stockport fiddler would have known,
As he busked there in the mall,
Bowing away, engrossed, impromptu, on his own,
For the drive of the tune, lift of it all.

Line 8, in 'Absent-mindedness in a Church Choir'.

NOTE

Page 35 – Hopkins at St Beuno's

Hopkins spent three years of his study for the priesthood at the Jesuit college of St Beuno's, inland from Rhyl, on a hill overlooking the Vale of Clwyd. It was there that he wrote 'The Wreck of the Deutschland' and several of his most famous poems, such as 'The Windhover'.

St Winefride's Well, at nearby Holywell, one of the most ancient and continuously visited pilgrimage sites in the country, was close to Hopkins's heart. In the chapter 'Welsh and Wells', Norman White's biography of the poet goes into this, quoting (on p.242) the journal:

The strong unfailing flow of the water and the chain of cures from year to year all those centuries took hold of my mind with wonder at the bounty of God in one of his saints, the sensible thing so naturally and gracefully uttering the spiritual reason of its being (which is all in true keeping with the story of St Winefride's death and recovery) and the spring in place leading back the thoughts by its spring in time to its spring in eternity; even now the stress and buoyancy and abundance of the water is before my eyes